I0006525

NIST Special Publication 800-27 Rev A

Engineering Principles for Information Technology Security (A Baseline for Achieving Security), Revision A

**Recommendations of the
National Institute of Standards and Technology**

Gary Stoneburner[1], Clark Hayden[2],
and Alexis Feringa[2]

C O M P U T E R   S E C U R I T Y

[1]Computer Security Division
Information Technology Laboratory
National Institute of Standards and Technology
Gaithersburg, MD 20899-8930

[2]Booz-Allen and Hamilton

June 2004

U.S. Department of Commerce
Donald L. Evans, Secretary

Technology Administration
Karen H. Brown, Acting Under Secretary of Commerce for Technology

National Institute of Standards and Technology
Karen H. Brown, Acting Director

Change History

Revision	Change
A	Updated "Authority" section
	Grouped principles into categories to facilitate use and understanding
	Deleted former Appendix A "IT specialist Positions" as being unnecessary
	Editorial changes largely due to comments received

Table of Contents

1.0 INTRODUCTION

1.1 Authority

This document has been developed by the National Institute of Standards and Technology (NIST) in furtherance of its statutory responsibilities under the Federal Information Security Management Act (FISMA) of 2002, Public Law 107-347.

NIST is responsible for developing standards and guidelines, including minimum requirements, for providing adequate information security for all agency operations and assets, but such standards and guidelines shall not apply to national security systems. This guideline is consistent with the requirements of the Office of Management and Budget (OMB) Circular A-130, Section 8b(3), Securing Agency Information Systems, as analyzed in A-130, Appendix IV: Analysis of Key Sections. Supplemental information is provided A-130, Appendix III.

This guideline has been prepared for use by federal agencies. It may be used by nongovernmental organizations on a voluntary basis and is not subject to copyright. (Attribution would be appreciated by NIST.)

Nothing in this document should be taken to contradict standards and guidelines made mandatory and binding on federal agencies by the Secretary of Commerce under statutory authority. Nor should these guidelines be interpreted as altering or superseding the existing authorities of the Secretary of Commerce, Director of the OMB, or any other federal official.

1.2 Purpose

The purpose of the Engineering Principles for Information Technology (IT) Security (EP-ITS) is to present a list of system-level security principles to be considered in the design, development, and operation of an information system.

> **Principle *n.*** – A rule or standard, especially of good behavior.
>
> American Heritage Dictionary

Ideally, the principles presented here would be used from the onset of a program—at the beginning of, or during the initiation phase—and then employed throughout the system's life-cycle. However, these principles are also helpful in affirming and confirming the security posture of already deployed information systems. The principles are short and concise and can be used by organizations to develop their system life-cycle policies.

1.3 Scope

This document is published by the National Institute of Standards and Technology (NIST) as recommended guidance for Federal departments and agencies and is intended to be usable by both the government and the private sector.

This document should be used by those interested in IT security and is applicable to all IT systems, including general support systems and major applications.

This document presents generic principles that apply to all systems. It is anticipated that the application of these generic principles to specific technology areas will be accomplished by use of this document in developing more detailed guidance.

1.4 Audience

The principles presented herein can be used by:

- **Users** when developing and evaluating functional requirements, or when operating information systems within their organizations.

- **System Engineers and Architects** when designing, implementing, or modifying an information system.

- **IT Specialists** during all phases of the system life-cycle.

- **Program Managers and Information System Security Officers (ISSO)** to ensure adequate security measures have been considered for all phases of the system life-cycle.

1.5 Document Structure

Section 1 of this document provided the purpose and scope, and clarified the intended audience.

Section 2 provides background information, including how this document is related to other NIST, Federal, and international documents and initiatives including *Generally Accepted Principles and Practices for Securing Information Technology Systems*, SP 800-14, September 1996; the Common Criteria; and layered-protections (also called "defense in depth").

Section 3, the main section of this document, presents 33 security principles and identifies their applicability in the life-cycle phases.

Section 4 is a short summary.

Appendix A defines terms used in this document.

Appendix B provides a list of referenced documents and other sources of information.

2.0   BACKGROUND

Private businesses and government agencies, both foreign and domestic, are becoming increasingly reliant on information technology to fulfill many basic functions. Businesses are making changes simply to remain competitive in the changing global marketplace. Likewise, government agencies are seeking to provide better service to their citizens.

Regardless of the reason, the move to a digital economy has caused information and information technology to become valuable business assets that need to be protected. With this development has come the recognition that fulfilling these basic functions requires as a matter of course comprehensive, well-designed, and reliable information system security programs.

Information system security program standards, guidance, and implementation strategies have been, or are being, developed by public and private sector organizations in the United States and abroad. These wide-ranging efforts are designed to address many aspects of information security at many levels of detail. They address technology aspects such as public key infrastructure (PKI) and certification and accreditation (C&A) processes, and more operational aspects such as organizational good practices.

Seeking to support and guide these many efforts, several private and public organizations have developed a number of explicit and implicit information system security principles. These security principles, in turn, have the potential to become common fundamentals for users, designers, and engineers to consider in designing information system security programs.

This document seeks to compile and present many of these security principles into one, easy-to-use document for those concerned with information system security. In contrast to other organization-level efforts, the principles presented in this document are structured around a system-level, engineering approach.

2.1   *Generally Accepted Principles and Practices for Securing Information Technology Systems* (SP 800-14)

SP 800-14 (available at http://csrc.nist.gov/publications/nistpubs/index.html) provides a foundation upon which organizations can establish and review information technology security programs. The eight Generally Accepted System Security Principles in SP 800-14 are designed to provide the public or private sector audience with an organization-level perspective when creating new systems, practices, or policies.

While derived primarily from concepts found in the eight principles and 14 practices identified in the SP 800-14, the EP-ITS principles provide a system-level (versus organizational-level) perspective for information technology security.

It should be noted the EP-ITS principles are not ordered under the same headings used in SP 800-14. This is due to the different focus for the two documents and is akin to the loose relationship between principles and practices that exists in SP 800-14.

2.2   Common Criteria

The Common Criteria (CC, available at http://www.commoncriteriaportal.org/) provides a structured methodology for documenting security requirements, documenting and validating security capabilities, and promoting international cooperation in the area of IT security.

Use of Common Criteria "protection profiles" and "security targets" greatly aids the development of products (and to some extent systems) that have IT security functions. The rigor and repeatability of the Common Criteria methodology provides for thorough definition of user security needs. Security targets provide system integrators with key information needed in the procurement of components and implementation of secure IT systems.   The approach of this document meshes with the Common Criteria methodology; EP-ITS provides system-level, broad principles and the CC provides a catalog of detailed, primarily product-level requirements.

2.3   Layered Protections

Securing information and systems against the full spectrum of threats requires the use of multiple, overlapping protection approaches addressing the people, technology, and operational aspects of information systems. This is due to the highly interactive nature of the various systems and networks, and the fact that any single system cannot be adequately secured unless all interconnecting systems are also secured.

By using multiple, overlapping protection approaches, the failure or circumvention of any individual protection approach will not leave the system unprotected. Through user training and awareness, well-crafted policies and procedures, and redundancy of protection mechanisms, layered protections enable effective protection of information technology for the purpose of achieving mission objectives.

For example, this fundamental need for layered protections is captured in the "Defense-in-Depth" strategy being used by DoD for protecting information systems. A source of information on implementing layered protections is the Information Assurance Technical Framework (IATF, http://www.iatf.net/). The IATF advocates the use of multiple information technology protection methods or approaches following the DoD "Defense-in-Depth" strategy to establish a composite security posture adequately addressing threats.

Federal agencies may find useful information in the IATF documents.

3.0 SECURITY PRINCIPLES

3.1 Introduction

To aid in designing a secure information system, NIST compiled a set of engineering principles for system security. These principles provide a foundation upon which a more consistent and structured approach to the design, development, and implementation of IT security capabilities can be constructed.

While the primary focus of these principles is the implementation of technical controls, these principles highlight the fact that, to be effective, a system security design should also consider non-technical issues, such as policy, operational procedures, and user education and training.

The principles described here do not apply to all systems at all times. Yet, each principle should be carefully considered throughout the life-cycle of every system. Moreover, because of the constantly changing information system security environment, the principles identified are not considered to be a static, all-inclusive list. Instead, this document is an attempt to present in a logical fashion fundamental security principles that can be used in today's operational environments. As technology improves and security techniques are refined, additions, deletions, and refinement of these security principles will be required.

Each principle has two components. The first is a table that indicates where the principle should be applied during the system life-cycle. The second is an explanatory narrative further amplifying the principle.

The five life-cycle planning phases used are defined in the *Generally Accepted Principles and Practices for Securing Information Technology Systems*, SP 800-14:

- Initiation Phase
- Development/Acquisition Phase
- Implementation Phase
- Operation/Maintenance Phase
- Disposal Phase.

In an effort to associate each principle with the relevant life-cycle planning phase(s), a table similar to the example table below, Table 3-1, has been developed for each principle. The table identifies each life-cycle phase, and "check marks" are used to indicate if the principle should be considered or applied during the specified phase. One check "✓" signifies the principle can be used to support the life-cycle phase, and two checks "✓✓" signifies the principle is key to successful completion of the life-cycle phase.

Table 3-1 Example Life-cycle Applicability Table

	Initiation	Devel/Acquis	Implement	Oper/Maint	Disposal
Principle X	✓✓	✓		✓	

For example, the table above indicates that Principle No. X *must* be considered and is key to the successful completion of the Initiation phase. Additionally, Principle No. X, *should* be considered and applied in support of the Development/Acquisition and the Operation/Maintenance phases.

3.2 System Life-Cycle Description

The following brief descriptions of each of the five phases of the system life-cycle are taken from *Generally Accepted Principles and Practices for Securing Information Technology Systems*, SP 800-14.

- **Initiation:** During the initiation phase, the need for a system is expressed and the purpose of the system is documented. Activities include conducting an impact assessment in accordance with FIPS-199 (http://csrc.nist.gov/publications/fips/fips199/FIPS-PUB-199-final.pdf).

- **Development/Acquisition:** During this phase, the system is designed, purchased, programmed, developed, or otherwise constructed. This phase often consists of other defined cycles, such as the system development cycle or the acquisition cycle. Activities include determining security requirements, incorporating security requirements into specifications, and obtaining the system.

- **Implementation:** During implementation, the system is tested and installed or fielded. Activities include installing/turning on controls, security testing, certification, and accreditation.

- **Operation/Maintenance:** During this phase, the system performs its work. Typically, the system is also being modified by the addition of hardware and software and by numerous other events. Activities include security operations and administration, operational assurance, and audits and monitoring.

- **Disposal:** The disposal phase of the IT system life-cycle involves the disposition of information, hardware, and software. Activities include moving, archiving, discarding or destroying information and sanitizing the media.

3.3 IT Security Principles

The 33 IT security principles are grouped into the following 6 categories: Security Foundation, Risk Based, Ease of Use, Increase Resilience, Reduce Vulnerabilities, and Design with Network in Mind. This grouping has resulted in a renumbering of the principles with respect to the original version of SP 800-27. The previous numbering is indicated to assist those familiar with the principles using the previous numbering.

3.3.1 <u>Security Foundation</u>

Principle 1.   Establish a sound security policy as the "foundation" for design.

	Initiation	Devel/Acquis	Implement	Oper/Maint	Disposal
Applicability	✓✓	✓	✓	✓	✓

Discussion: A security policy is an important document to develop while designing an information system. The security policy begins with the organization's basic commitment to information security formulated as a general policy statement. The policy is then applied to all aspects of the system design or security solution. The policy identifies security goals (e.g., confidentiality, integrity, availability, accountability, and assurance) the system should support, and these goals guide the procedures, standards and controls used in the IT security architecture design. The policy also should require definition of critical assets, the perceived threat, and security-related roles and responsibilities.

Principle 2.   Treat security as an integral part of the overall system design.

	Initiation	Devel/Acquis	Implement	Oper/Maint	Disposal
Applicability	✓✓	✓✓	✓✓	✓✓	✓

Discussion: Security must be considered in information system design. Experience has shown it to be both difficult and costly to implement security measures properly and successfully after a system has been developed, so it should be integrated fully into the system life-cycle process. This includes establishing security policies, understanding the resulting security requirements, participating in the evaluation of security products, and finally in the engineering, design, implementation, and disposal of the system.

Principle 3.   Clearly delineate the physical and logical security boundaries governed by associated security policies.

	Initiation	Devel/Acquis	Implement	Oper/Maint	Disposal
Applicability	✓✓	✓✓	✓	✓	

Discussion: Information technology exists in physical and logical locations, and boundaries exist between these locations. An understanding of what is to be protected from external factors can help ensure adequate protective measures are applied where they will be most effective. Sometimes a boundary is defined by people, information, and information technology associated with one physical location. But this ignores the reality that, within a single location, many different security policies may be in place, some covering publicly accessible information and some covering sensitive unclassified information. Other times a boundary is defined by a security policy that governs a specific set of information and information technology that can cross physical boundaries. Further complicating the matter is that, many times, a single machine or server may house both public-access and sensitive unclassified information. As a result, multiple security policies may apply to a single machine or within a single system. Therefore, when developing an information system, security boundaries must be considered and communicated in relevant system documentation and security policies.

Principle 4 (formerly 33).	*Ensure that developers are trained in how to develop secure software.*

	Initiation	Devel/Acquis	Implement	Oper/Maint	Disposal
Applicability	✓✓	✓✓	✓		

Discussion: It is unwise to assume that developers know how to develop secure software. Therefore, ensure that developers are adequately trained in the development of secure software before developing the system. This includes application of engineering disciplines to design, development, configuration control, and integration and testing.

3.3.2 Risk Based

Principle 5 (formerly 4).	*Reduce risk to an acceptable level.*

	Initiation	Devel/Acquis	Implement	Oper/Maint	Disposal
Applicability	✓✓	✓✓	✓✓	✓✓	✓✓

Discussion: Risk is defined as the combination of (1) the likelihood that a particular threat source will exercise (intentionally exploit or unintentionally trigger) a particular information system vulnerability and (2) the resulting adverse impact on organizational operations, organizational assets, or individuals should this occur. Previously, risk avoidance was a common IT security goal. That changed as the nature of the risk became better understood. Today, it is recognized that elimination of all risk is not cost-effective. A cost-benefit analysis should be conducted for each proposed control. In some cases, the benefits of a more secure system may not justify the direct and indirect costs. Benefits include more than just prevention of monetary loss; for example, controls may be essential for maintaining public trust and confidence. Direct costs include the cost of purchasing and installing a given technology; indirect costs include decreased system performance and additional training. The goal is to enhance mission/business capabilities by mitigating mission/business risk to an acceptable level. (Related Principle: 6)

Principle 6 (formerly 5).	*Assume that external systems are insecure.*

	Initiation	Devel/Acquis	Implement	Oper/Maint	Disposal
Applicability	✓✓	✓✓	✓✓	✓✓	✓

Discussion: The term information domain arises from the practice of partitioning information resources according to access control, need, and levels of protection required. Organizations implement specific measures to enforce this partitioning and to provide for the deliberate flow of authorized information between information domains. The boundary of an information domain represents the security perimeter for that domain.

An external domain is one that is not under your control. In general, external systems should be considered insecure. Until an external domain has been deemed "trusted," system engineers, architects, and IT specialists should presume the security measures of an external system are different than those of a trusted internal system and design the system security features accordingly.

Principle 7 (formerly 6).   Identify potential trade-offs between reducing risk and increased costs and decrease in other aspects of operational effectiveness.

	Initiation	Devel/Acquis	Implement	Oper/Maint	Disposal
Applicability	✓✓	✓✓		✓✓	

Discussion: To meet stated security requirements, a systems designer, architect, or security practitioner will need to identify and address all competing operational needs. It may be necessary to modify or adjust (i.e., trade-off) security goals due to other operational requirements. In modifying or adjusting security goals, an acceptance of greater risk and cost may be inevitable. By identifying and addressing these trade-offs as early as possible, decision makers will have greater latitude and be able to achieve more effective systems. (Related Principle: 4)

Principle 8.   Implement tailored system security measures to meet organizational security goals.

	Initiation	Devel/Acquis	Implement	Oper/Maint	Disposal
Applicability	✓	✓✓	✓	✓✓	✓

Discussion: In general, IT security measures are tailored according to an organization's unique needs. While numerous factors, such as the overriding mission requirements, and guidance, are to be considered, the fundamental issue is the protection of the mission or business from IT security-related, negative impacts. Because IT security needs are not uniform, system designers and security practitioners should consider the level of trust when connecting to other external networks and internal sub-domains. Recognizing the uniqueness of each system allows a layered security strategy to be used – implementing lower assurance solutions with lower costs to protect less critical systems and higher assurance solutions only at the most critical areas.

Principle 9 (formerly 26).   Protect information while being processed, in transit, and in storage.

	Initiation	Devel/Acquis	Implement	Oper/Maint	Disposal
Applicability	✓	✓✓	✓	✓✓	✓

Discussion: The risk of unauthorized modification or destruction of data, disclosure of information, and denial of access to data while in transit should be considered along with the risks associated with data that is in storage or being processed. Therefore, system engineers, architects, and IT specialists should implement security measures to preserve, as needed, the integrity, confidentiality, and availability of data, including application software, while the information is being processed, in transit, and in storage.

Principle 10 (formerly 29).   Consider custom products to achieve adequate security.

	Initiation	Devel/Acquis	Implement	Oper/Maint	Disposal
Applicability	✓	✓✓	✓	✓	

Discussion: Designers should recognize that in some instances it will not be possible to meet security goals with systems constructed entirely from COTS products. In such instances, it will be necessary to augment COTS with non-COTS mechanisms.

Principle 11 (formerly 31).   Protect against all likely classes of "attacks."

	Initiation	Devel/Acquis	Implement	Oper/Maint	Disposal
Applicability	✓	✓✓	✓	✓	✓

Discussion: In designing the security controls, multiple classes of "attacks" need to be considered. Those classes that result in unacceptable risk need to be mitigated. Examples of "attack" classes are: Passive monitoring, active network attacks, exploitation by insiders, attacks requiring physical access or proximity, and the insertion of backdoors and malicious code during software development and/or distribution.

3.3.3 Ease of Use

Principle 12 (formerly 18).   Where possible, base security on open standards for portability and interoperability.

	Initiation	Devel/Acquis	Implement	Oper/Maint	Disposal
Applicability	✓	✓✓	✓		

Discussion: Most organizations depend significantly on distributed information systems to perform their mission or business. These systems distribute information both across their own organization and to other organizations. For security capabilities to be effective in such environments, security program designers should make every effort to incorporate interoperability and portability into all security measures, including hardware and software, and implementation practices.

Principle 13 (formerly 19).   Use common language in developing security requirements.

	Initiation	Devel/Acquis	Implement	Oper/Maint	Disposal
Applicability	✓✓	✓✓		✓✓	

Discussion: The use of a common language when developing security requirements permits organizations to evaluate and compare security products and features evaluated in a common test environment. When a "common" evaluation process is based upon common requirements or criteria, a level of confidence can be established that ensures product security functions conform to an organization's security requirements. The Common Criteria provides a source of common expressions for common needs and supports a common assessment methodology.

Principle 14 (formerly 21). Design security to allow for regular adoption of new technology, including a secure and logical technology upgrade process.

	Initiation	Devel/Acquis	Implement	Oper/Maint	Disposal
Applicability		✓✓	✓	✓✓	

Discussion: As mission and business processes and the threat environment change, security requirements and technical protection methods must be updated. IT-related risks to the mission/business vary over time and undergo periodic assessment. Periodic assessment should be performed to enable system designers and managers to make informed risk management decisions on whether to accept or mitigate identified risks with changes or updates to the security capability. The lack of timely identification through consistent security solution re-evaluation and correction of evolving, applicable IT vulnerabilities results in false trust and increased risk.

Each security mechanism should be able to support migration to new technology or upgrade of new features without requiring an entire system redesign. The security design should be modular so that individual parts of the security design can be upgraded without the requirement to modify the entire system.

Principle 15 (formerly 27). Strive for operational ease of use.

	Initiation	Devel/Acquis	Implement	Oper/Maint	Disposal
Applicability	✓	✓✓	✓	✓✓	

Discussion: The more difficult it is to maintain and operate a security control, the less effective that control is likely to be. Therefore, security controls should be designed to be consistent with the concept of operations and with ease-of-use as an important consideration. The experience and expertise of administrators and users should be appropriate and proportional to the operation of the security control. An organization must invest the resources necessary to ensure system administrators and users are properly trained. Moreover, administrator and user training costs along with the life-cycle operational costs should be considered when determining the cost-effectiveness of the security control.

3.3.4 Increase Resilience

Principle 16 (formerly 7). *Implement layered security (Ensure no single point of vulerability).*

	Initiation	Devel/Acquis	Implement	Oper/Maint	Disposal
Applicability	✓	✓✓	✓	✓✓	✓

Discussion: Security designs should consider a layered approach to address or protect against a specific threat or to reduce vulnerability. For example, the use of a packet-filtering router in conjunction with an application gateway and an intrusion detection system combine to increase the work-factor an attacker must expend to successfully attack the system. Adding good password controls and adequate user training improves the system's security posture even more.

The need for layered protections is especially important when commercial-off-the-shelf (COTS) products are used. Practical experience has shown that the current state-of-the-art for security quality in COTS products does not provide a high degree of protection against sophisticated attacks. It is possible to help mitigate this situation by placing several controls in series, requiring additional work by attackers to accomplish their goals.

Principle 17 (formerly 10). *Design and operate an IT system to limit damage and to be resilient in response.*

	Initiation	Devel/Acquis	Implement	Oper/Maint	Disposal
Applicability	✓	✓✓		✓✓	

Discussion: Information systems should be resistant to attack, should limit damage, and should recover rapidly when attacks do occur. The principle suggested here recognizes the need for adequate protection technologies at all levels to ensure that any potential cyber attack will be countered effectively. There are vulnerabilities that cannot be fixed, those that have not yet been fixed, those that are not known, and those that could be fixed but are not (e.g., risky services allowed through firewalls) to allow increased operational capabilities. In addition to achieving a secure initial state, secure systems should have a well-defined status after failure, either to a secure failure state or via a recovery procedure to a known secure state. Organizations should establish detect and respond capabilities, manage single points of failure in their systems, and implement a reporting and response strategy. (Related Principle: 14)

	Initiation	Devel/Acquis	Implement	Oper/Maint	Disposal
Applicability	✓	✓✓	✓	✓✓	✓

Discussion: Assurance is the grounds for confidence that a system meets its security expectations. These expectations can typically be summarized as providing sufficient resistance to both direct penetration and attempts to circumvent security controls. Good understanding of the threat environment, evaluation of requirement sets, hardware and software engineering disciplines, and product and system evaluations are primary measures used to achieve assurance. Additionally, the documentation of the specific and evolving threats is important in making timely adjustments in applied security and strategically supporting incremental security enhancements.

Principle 19 (formerly 14). Limit or contain vulnerabilities.

	Initiation	Devel/Acquis	Implement	Oper/Maint	Disposal
Applicability		✓✓	✓	✓	

Discussion: Design systems to limit or contain vulnerabilities. If a vulnerability does exist, damage can be limited or contained, allowing other information system elements to function properly. Limiting and containing insecurities also helps to focus response and reconstitution efforts to information system areas most in need. (Related Principle: 10)

Principle 20 (formerly 16). Isolate public access systems from mission critical resources (e.g., data, processes, etc.).

	Initiation	Devel/Acquis	Implement	Oper/Maint	Disposal
Applicability	✓	✓✓	✓	✓	

Discussion: While the trend toward shared infrastructure has considerable merit in many cases, it is not universally applicable. In cases where the sensitivity or criticality of the information is high, organizations may want to limit the number of systems on which that data is stored and isolate them, either physically or logically. Physical isolation may include ensuring that no physical connection exists between an organization's public access information resources and an organization's critical information. When implementing logical isolation solutions, layers of security services and mechanisms should be established between public systems and secure systems responsible for protecting mission critical resources. Security layers may include using network architecture designs such as demilitarized zones and screened subnets. Finally, system designers and administrators should enforce organizational security policies and procedures regarding use of public access systems.

Principle 21 (formerly 17). Use boundary mechanisms to separate computing systems and network infrastructures.

	Initiation	Devel/Acquis	Implement	Oper/Maint	Disposal
Applicability		✓✓	✓	✓✓	

Discussion: To control the flow of information and access across network boundaries in computing and communications infrastructures, and to enforce the proper separation of user groups, a suite of access control devices and accompanying access control policies should be used.

Determine the following for communications across network boundaries:

- What external interfaces are required
- Whether information is pushed or pulled
- What ports, protocols, and network services are required
- What requirements exist for system information exchanges; for example, trust relationships, database replication services, and domain name resolution processes.

Principle 22 (formerly 20). Design and implement audit mechanisms to detect unauthorized use and to support incident investigations.

	Initiation	Devel/Acquis	Implement	Oper/Maint	Disposal
Applicability	✓	✓✓	✓✓	✓	

Discussion: Organizations should monitor, record, and periodically review audit logs to identify unauthorized use and to ensure system resources are functioning properly. In some cases, organizations may be required to disclose information obtained through auditing mechanisms to appropriate third parties, including law enforcement authorities or Freedom of Information Act (FOIA) applicants. Many organizations have implemented consent to monitor policies which state that evidence of unauthorized use (e.g., audit trails) may be used to support administrative or criminal investigations.

Principle 23 (formerly 28). Develop and exercise contingency or disaster recovery procedures to ensure appropriate availability.

	Initiation	Devel/Acquis	Implement	Oper/Maint	Disposal
Applicability	✓	✓	✓	✓✓	

Discussion: Continuity of operations plans or disaster recovery procedures address continuance of an organization's operation in the event of a disaster or prolonged service interruption that affects the organization's mission. Such plans should address an emergency response phase, a recovery phase, and a return to normal operation phase. Personnel responsibilities during an incident and available resources should be identified. In reality, contingency and disaster recovery plans do not address every possible scenario or assumption. Rather, it focuses on the events most likely to occur and identifies an acceptable method of recovery. Periodically, the plans and procedures should be exercised to ensure that they are effective and well understood.

3.3.5 Reduce Vulnerabilities

Principle 24 (formerly 9).   Strive for simplicity.

	Initiation	Devel/Acquis	Implement	Oper/Maint	Disposal
Applicability	✓	✓✓	✓	✓✓	

Discussion: The more complex the mechanism, the more likely it may possess exploitable flaws. Simple mechanisms tend to have fewer exploitable flaws and require less maintenance. Further, because configuration management issues are simplified, updating or replacing a simple mechanism becomes a less intensive process.

Principle 25 (formerly 11).   Minimize the system elements to be trusted.

	Initiation	Devel/Acquis	Implement	Oper/Maint	Disposal
Applicability	✓	✓✓	✓	✓✓	

Discussion: Security measures include people, operations, and technology. Where technology is used, hardware, firmware, and software should be designed and implemented so that a minimum number of system elements need to be trusted in order to maintain protection. Further, to ensure cost-effective and timely certification of system security features, it is important to minimize the amount of software and hardware expected to provide the most secure functions for the system.

Principle 26 (formerly 24). Implement least privilege.

	Initiation	Devel/Acquis	Implement	Oper/Maint	Disposal
Applicability	✓	✓	✓	✓✓	

Discussion:

The concept of limiting access, or "least privilege," is simply to provide no more authorizations than necessary to perform required functions. This is perhaps most often applied in the administration of the system. Its goal is to reduce risk by limiting the number of people with access to critical system security controls; i.e., controlling who is allowed to enable or disable system security features or change the privileges of users or programs. Best practice suggests it is better to have several administrators with limited access to security resources rather than one person with "super user" permissions. .

Consideration should be given to implementing role-based access controls for various aspects of system use, not only administration. The system security policy can identify and define the various roles of users or processes. Each role is assigned those permissions needed to perform its functions. Each permission specifies a permitted access to a particular resource (such as "read" and "write" access to a specified file or directory, "connect" access to a given host and port, etc.). Unless a permission is granted explicitly, the user or process should not be able to access the protected resource. Additionally, identify the roles/responsibilities that, for security purposes, should remain separate, this is commonly termed "separation of duties".

Principle 27 (formerly 25). Do not implement unnecessary security mechanisms.

	Initiation	Devel/Acquis	Implement	Oper/Maint	Disposal
Applicability	✓	✓✓	✓✓	✓	✓

Discussion: Every security mechanism should support a security service or set of services, and every security service should support one or more security goals. Extra measures should not be implemented if they do not support a recognized service or security goal. Such mechanisms could add unneeded complexity to the system and are potential sources of additional vulnerabilities.

An example is file encryption supporting the access control service that in turn supports the goals of confidentiality and integrity by preventing unauthorized file access. If file encryption is a necessary part of accomplishing the goals, then the mechanism is appropriate. However, if these security goals are adequately supported without inclusion of file encryption, then that mechanism would be an unneeded system complexity.

Principle 28 (formerly 30). Ensure proper security in the shutdown or disposal of a system.

	Initiation	Devel/Acquis	Implement	Oper/Maint	Disposal
Applicability		✓		✓	✓✓

Discussion: Although a system may be powered down, critical information still resides on the system and could be retrieved by an unauthorized user or organization. Access to critical information systems must be controlled at all times.

At the end of a system's life-cycle, system designers should develop procedures to dispose of an information system's assets in a proper and secure fashion. Procedures must be implemented to ensure system hard drives, volatile memory, and other media are purged to an acceptable level and do not retain residual information.

Principle 29 (formerly 32). Identify and prevent common errors and vulnerabilities.

	Initiation	Devel/Acquis	Implement	Oper/Maint	Disposal
Applicability		✓✓	✓✓	✓	

Discussion: Many errors reoccur with disturbing regularity - errors such as buffer overflows, race conditions, format string errors, failing to check input for validity, and programs being given excessive privileges. Learning from the past will improve future results.

3.3.6 Design with Network in Mind

Principle 30 (formerly 12). Implement security through a combination of measures distributed physically and logically.

	Initiation	Devel/Acquis	Implement	Oper/Maint	Disposal
Applicability		✓✓	✓	✓	✓

Discussion: Often, a single security service is achieved by cooperating elements existing on separate machines. For example, system authentication is typically accomplished using elements ranging from the user-interface on a workstation through the networking elements to an application on an authentication server. It is important to associate all elements with the security service they provide. These components are likely to be shared across systems to achieve security as infrastructure resources come under more senior budget and operational control.

Principle 31 (formerly 15).   Formulate security measures to address multiple overlapping information domains.

	Initiation	Devel/Acquis	Implement	Oper/Maint	Disposal
Applicability	✓	✓✓	✓	✓	

Discussion: An information domain is a set of active entities (person, process, or devices) and their data objects. A single information domain may be subject to multiple security policies. A single security policy may span multiple information domains. An efficient and cost effective security capability should be able to enforce multiple security policies to protect multiple information domains without the need to separate physically the information and respective information systems processing the data. This principle argues for moving away from the traditional practice of creating separate LANs and infrastructures for various sensitivity levels (e.g., security classification or business function such as proposal development) and moving toward solutions that enable the use of common, shared, infrastructures with appropriate protections at the operating system, application, and workstation level.

Moreover, to accomplish missions and protect critical functions, government and private sector organizations have many types of information to safeguard. With this principle in mind, system engineers, architects, and IT specialists should develop a security capability that allows organizations with multiple levels of information sensitivity to achieve the basic security goals in an efficient manner.

Principle 32 (formerly 22).   Authenticate users and processes to ensure appropriate access control decisions both within and across domains.

	Initiation	Devel/Acquis	Implement	Oper/Maint	Disposal
Applicability	✓	✓	✓	✓✓	

Discussion: Authentication is the process where a system establishes the validity of a transmission, message, or a means of verifying the eligibility of an individual, process, or machine to carry out a desired action, thereby ensuring that security is not compromised by an untrusted source. It is essential that adequate authentication be achieved in order to implement security policies and achieve security goals. Additionally, level of trust is always an issue when dealing with cross-domain interactions. The solution is to establish an authentication policy and apply it to cross-domain interactions as required. Note: A user may have rights to use more than one name in multiple domains. Further, rights may differ among the domains, potentially leading to security policy violations.

Principle 33 (formerly 23). Use unique identities to ensure accountability.

	Initiation	Devel/Acquis	Implement	Oper/Maint	Disposal
Applicability	✓	✓	✓	✓✓	

Discussion: An identity may represent an actual user or a process with its own identity, e.g., a program making a remote access. Unique identities are a required element in order to be able to:

- Maintain accountability and traceability of a user or process
- Assign specific rights to an individual user or process
- Provide for non-repudiation
- Enforce access control decisions
- Establish the identity of a peer in a secure communications path
- Prevent unauthorized users from masquerading as an authorized user.

3.4   Principle/Life-cycle Summary

Table 3-2 below summarizes the relationship between the 33 principles above and the life-cycles to which they apply.

Table 3-2: Principles versus Life-Cycles

Principle	Life-Cycle Applicability				
	Initiation	Devel/Acquis	Implement	Oper/Maint	Disposal
1	✓✓	✓	✓	✓	✓
2	✓✓	✓✓	✓✓	✓✓	✓
3	✓✓	✓✓	✓	✓	
4 (formerly 33)	✓✓	✓✓	✓		
5 (formerly 4)	✓✓	✓✓	✓✓	✓✓	✓✓
6 (formerly 5)	✓✓	✓✓	✓✓	✓✓	✓
7 (formerly 6)	✓✓	✓✓		✓✓	
8	✓	✓✓	✓	✓✓	✓
9 (formerly 26)	✓	✓✓	✓	✓✓	✓
10 (formerly 29)	✓	✓✓	✓	✓	
11 (formerly 31)	✓	✓✓	✓✓	✓	✓
12 (formerly 18)	✓	✓✓	✓		
13 (formerly 19)	✓✓	✓✓		✓✓	
14 (formerly 21)		✓✓	✓	✓✓	
15 (formerly 27)	✓	✓✓	✓	✓✓	
16 (formerly 7)	✓	✓✓	✓	✓✓	✓
17 (formerly 10)	✓	✓✓		✓✓	
18 (formerly 13)	✓	✓✓	✓	✓✓	✓
19 (formerly 14)		✓✓	✓	✓	
20 (formerly 16)	✓	✓✓	✓	✓	
21 (formerly 17)		✓✓	✓	✓✓	
22 (formerly 20)	✓	✓✓	✓✓	✓	
23 (formerly 28)	✓	✓	✓	✓✓	
24 (formerly 9)	✓	✓✓	✓	✓✓	
25 (formerly 11)	✓	✓✓	✓	✓✓	
26 (formerly 24)	✓	✓	✓	✓✓	
27 (formerly 25)	✓	✓	✓	✓	✓
28 (formerly 30)		✓		✓	✓✓
29 (formerly 32)		✓✓	✓✓	✓	
30 (formerly 12)		✓✓	✓	✓	✓
31 (formerly 15)	✓	✓✓	✓	✓	
32 (formerly 22)	✓	✓	✓	✓✓	
33 (formerly 23)	✓	✓	✓	✓✓	

4.0   SUMMARY

Now, more than ever, IT security is a critical element in the system life-cycle. Security must be incorporated and addressed from the initial planning and design phases to disposal of the system. Without proper attention to security, an organization's information technology can become a source of significant mission risks. With careful planning from the earliest stages, however, security becomes an enabler, supporting and helping to achieve the organization's mission.

As security awareness becomes a way of life within an organization, people at all levels, and roles in the system life-cycle, should have access to easily understood guidance. From users to system administrators and program managers, everyone should have a basic understanding of the security principles governing the system they are using, maintaining, or designing and developing.

This document provides a starting point. The principles contained herein are derived from a number of national and international documents, as well as from the experience of the scientists at NIST. It is hoped that these principles will contribute to improved IT security in any organization.

APPENDIX A – DEFINITIONS

Term	Definition
access control	Enable authorized use of a resource while preventing unauthorized use or use in an unauthorized manner.
accountability	The security goal that generates the requirement for actions of an entity to be traced uniquely to that entity. This supports non-repudiation, deterrence, fault isolation, intrusion detection and prevention, and after-action recovery and legal action.
assurance	Grounds for confidence that the other four security goals (integrity, availability, confidentiality, and accountability) have been adequately met by a specific implementation. "Adequately met" includes (1) functionality that performs correctly, (2) sufficient protection against unintentional errors (by users or software), and (3) sufficient resistance to intentional penetration or by-pass.
authentication	Verifying the identity of a user, process, or device, often as a prerequisite to allowing access to resources in a system.
authorization	The granting or denying of access rights to a user, program, or process.
availability	The security goal that generates the requirement for protection against intentional or accidental attempts to (1) perform unauthorized deletion of data or (2) otherwise cause a denial of service or data.
confidentiality	The security goal that generates the requirement for protection from intentional or accidental attempts to perform unauthorized data reads. Confidentiality covers data in storage, during processing, and while in transit.
data integrity	The property that data has not been altered in an unauthorized manner. Data integrity covers data in storage, during processing, and while in transit.
denial of service	The prevention of authorized access to resources or the delaying of time-critical operations. (Time-critical may be milliseconds or it may be hours, depending upon the service provided.)
domain	See security domain.

entity	Either a subject (an active element that operates on information or the system state) or an object (a passive element that contains or receives information).
general support system	An interconnected information resource under the same direct management control that shares common functionality. It normally includes hardware, software, information, data, applications, communications, facilities, and people and provides support for a variety of users and/or applications. Individual applications support different mission-related functions. Users may be from the same or different organizations.
integrity	The security goal that generates the requirement for protection against either intentional or accidental attempts to violate data integrity (the property that data has not been altered in an unauthorized manner) or system integrity (the quality that a system has when it performs its intended function in an unimpaired manner, free from unauthorized manipulation).
identity	Information that is unique within a security domain and which is recognized as denoting a particular entity within that domain.
IT-related risk	The net mission/business impact considering (1) the likelihood that a particular threat source will exploit, or trigger, a particular information system vulnerability and (2) the resulting impact if this should occur. IT-related risks arise from legal liability or mission/business loss due to, but not limited to: 1. Unauthorized (malicious, non-malicious, or accidental) disclosure, modification, or destruction of information. 2. Non-malicious errors and omissions. 3. IT disruptions due to natural or man-made disasters. 4. Failure to exercise due care and diligence in the implementation and operation of the IT.
IT security architecture	A description of security principles and an overall approach for complying with the principles that drive the system design; i.e., guidelines on the placement and implementation of specific security services within various distributed computing environments.
IT security goal	See "Security goal."

major application	An application that requires special attention to security due to the risk and magnitude of the harm resulting from the loss, misuse, or unauthorized access to, or modification of, the information in the application. A breach in a major application might comprise many individual application programs and hardware, software, and telecommunications components. Major applications can be either major software applications or a combination of hardware/software where the only purpose of the system is to support a specific mission-related function.
object	A passive entity that contains or receives information. Note that access to an object potentially implies access to the information it contains.
risk	Within this document, synonymous with "IT-related risk."
risk analysis	The process of identifying the risks to system security and determining the likelihood of occurrence, the resulting impact, and the additional safeguards that mitigate this impact. Part of risk management and synonymous with risk assessment.
risk assessment	See risk analysis.
risk management	The ongoing process of assessing the risk to mission/business as part of a risk-based approach used to determine adequate security for a system by analyzing the threats and vulnerabilities and selecting appropriate, cost-effective controls to achieve and maintain an acceptable level or risk.
security	Security is a system property. Security is much more than a set of functions and mechanisms. IT security is a system characteristic as well as a set of mechanisms that span the system both logically and physically.
security domain	A set of subjects, their information objects, and a common security policy.
security policy	The statement of required protection of the information objects.
security goals	The five security goals are confidentiality, availability, integrity, accountability, and assurance.
security service	A capability that supports one, or many, of the security goals. Examples of security services are key management, access control, and authentication.
subject	An active entity, generally in the form of a person, process, or device, that causes information to flow among objects or changes the system state.

system integrity	The quality that a system has when it performs its intended function in an unimpaired manner, free from unauthorized manipulation of the system, whether intentional or accidental.
threat	Any circumstance or event with the potential to harm an information system through unauthorized access, destruction, disclosure, modification of data, and/or denial of service. Threats arise from human actions and natural events.
threat source	Either (1) intent and method targeted at the intentional exploitation of a vulnerability or (2) the situation and method that may accidentally trigger a vulnerability.
threat analysis	The examination of threat sources against system vulnerabilities to determine the threats for a particular system in a particular operational environment.
vulnerability	A weakness in system security requirements, design, implementation, or operation, that could be accidentally triggered or intentionally exploited and result in a violation of the system's security policy.

APPENDIX B – REFERENCES AND OTHER SOURCES OF INFORMATION

Common Criteria for Information Technology Security Evaluation (CC), Version 2.2, (Version 2.1, August 1999, with interpretations through December 2003 applied). http://www.commoncriteriaportal.org/public/consumer/index.php?menu=2

Federal Information Processing Standard 199, *Standards for Security Categorization of Federal Information and Information Systems*, FIPS-199, February 2004. http://csrc.nist.gov/publications/fips/fips199/FIPS-PUB-199-final.pdf

Information Assurance Technical Framework (IATF), Release 3.0, October 2000. http://www.iatf.net/, member-only area, site registration at: https://www.iatf.net/register/

Management of Federal Information Resources, Circular A-130, Office of Management and Budget (OMB). http://www.whitehouse.gov/omb/circulars/a130/a130trans4.html

CNSS Instruction No. 4009, *National Information Assurance Glossary,* Revised May 2003. http://www.nstissc.gov/Assets/pdf/4009.pdf. While the majority of CNSSI-4009 definitions are used, some of the definitions in Appendix A have been determined to be more appropriate to the task of defining a technical baseline for IT security than similar definitions in CNSSI-4009.

Special Publications by National Institute of Standards and Technology (NIST) available at http://csrc.nist.gov/publications/nistpubs/index.html:

SP 800-12, *An Introduction to Computer Security: The NIST Handbook*, October 1995.

SP 800-14, *Generally Accepted Principles and Practices for Securing Information Technology Systems*, September 1996.

SP 800-16, *Information Technology Security Training Requirements: A Role and Performance-Base Model*, April 1998.

SP 800-18, *Guide for Developing Security Plans for Information Technology Systems*, December 1998.

SP 800-30 Rev A, *Risk Management Guide for Information Systems*, April 2004.

SP 800-31, *Intrusion Detection Systems (IDS)*, November 2001.

SP 800-33, *Underlying Technical Models for Information Technology Security*, December 2001.

SP 800-34, *Contingency Planning Guide for Information Technology Systems*, June 2002.

SP 800-35, *Guide to Information Technology Security Services*, October 2003.

SP 800-36, *Guide to Selecting Information Security Products*, October 2003.

SP 800-40, *Procedure for Handling Security Patches*, September 2002.

SP 800-41, *Guidelines on Firewalls and Firewall Policy*, SP 800-41 January 2002.

SP 800-47, *Security Guide for Interconnecting Information Technology Systems*, September 2002.

SP 800-50, *Building an Information Technology Security Awareness and Training Program*, October 2003.

SP 800-59, *Guideline for Identifying an Information System as a National Security System*, August 2003.

SP 800-61, *Computer Security Incident Handling Guide*, January 2004.

SP 800-64, *Security Considerations in the Information System Development Life Cycle*, October 2003.

www.ingramcontent.com/pod-product-compliance
Lightning Source LLC
Chambersburg PA
CBHW060513060326

40689CB00020B/4726